There Once Was a Man Called Adam

ISBN 978-1-63961-079-2 (paperback)
ISBN 978-1-63961-080-8 (digital)

Copyright © 2021 by Susan Greer

All rights reserved. No part of this publication may be reproduced, distributed, or transmitted in any form or by any means, including photocopying, recording, or other electronic or mechanical methods without the prior written permission of the publisher. For permission requests, solicit the publisher via the address below.

Christian Faith Publishing, Inc.
832 Park Avenue
Meadville, PA 16335
www.christianfaithpublishing.com

Printed in the United States of America

There Once Was a Man Called Adam

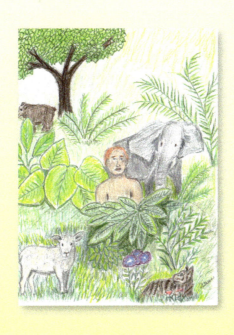

Susan Greer

There once was a man named Adam who lived in a garden called Eden. He had a wife called Eve. They were like children, pure and innocent.

Every day they would play and work in the garden.

In the cool of the day, their Father would come and walk with them. This was the best part of the day. They loved their Father, and he loved them.

Just as fathers do, he had made a rule: "You can eat any fruit in the garden but from this one tree."

You see, he wanted to test how good they could be.

One day a serpent was in that tree and told Eve to come and eat. She said no but didn't go. The serpent said, "Why not?" He twisted the Father's words and deceived her. She ate the fruit and gave it to Adam, and he did eat.

They lost their purity that day. They knew they had done wrong. They were no longer innocent.

The Father came in the cool of the day. Something was wrong. They had no song. They were afraid and hid. Fig leaf clothes they made to wear. To be seen naked they could not bear. The Father called them, and something was wrong. He was sad. He was angry. He loved them so. He shed the blood of an animal and made them clothes. Then he said, "You must go." So they went from the garden. Their way of life it did harden.

The Father said he would make a way by shed blood so they could come and walk with him again.

And so it was. Sacrifices were made by shedding animal blood to obtain forgiveness.

Through the years, the Father worked a plan so he could fellowship with man. Thousands of years did pass, and the children of Adam and Eve filled the earth with their sin.

The ultimate sacrifice must be made, and so a virgin had a son from the seed of the Father. He was pure. He was innocent. His blood was perfect. He knew no sin. She called him Jesus. He would be the last sacrifice the children would need.

So he grew in wisdom and stature—pure and innocent, the perfect Son., the only one who could make things right.

He was thirty and left his home the country to roam. He found twelve men to follow him. He taught them and told them what he must do. They said, "No, not you."

The dreaded day came at thirty-three. They took him away, the price to pay. He would die for every wrong from Adam and Eve and all their seed from that day to this.

So a cross he was put upon. He died for you and died for me. His blood was shed as the Father had said. It would wash away the sin and shame.

So it was. His deed was done. The innocent did die, but that's not the end. He went to hell where the serpent dwells. The serpent had brought the sin, the death, the trouble upon the earth. He had deceived the woman and taken the keys of life and death. Jesus took them back so no more would man have to suffer the effect of sin nor would he have to die forever. No more sickness, death, or pain—that was defeated when Jesus was slain.

So he ascended out of that hell with the keys to free me and you.

"What's that?" you say. Why didn't Eden return that day? Man had to make the choice to listen: to hear the voice of sin or hear the word and receive the gift of sacrifice. Since that day, man must choose the way that he should go. So it comes to this: let Jesus's life be your sacrifice or die the death of unforgiveness. Forgiveness is yours. You must choose. Ask Jesus to be your sacrifice. He died for you. Just ask him in. Proclaim your sin and ask to be forgiven. He will do it. Live for him. From this day on, walk with the Father, who is God.

About the Author

Susan Greer was born in Chicago and grew up in the northwest suburbs. Her faith and family are the two most important things in her life. She enjoys meeting people and sharing Jesus with them. Susan has been a Sunday school teacher for over fifty years. She shares the gospel everywhere with red hearts that say Jesus loves you and John 3:16 on them.

CPSIA information can be obtained
at www.ICGtesting.com
Printed in the USA
JSHW011340080222
22695JS00003B/59